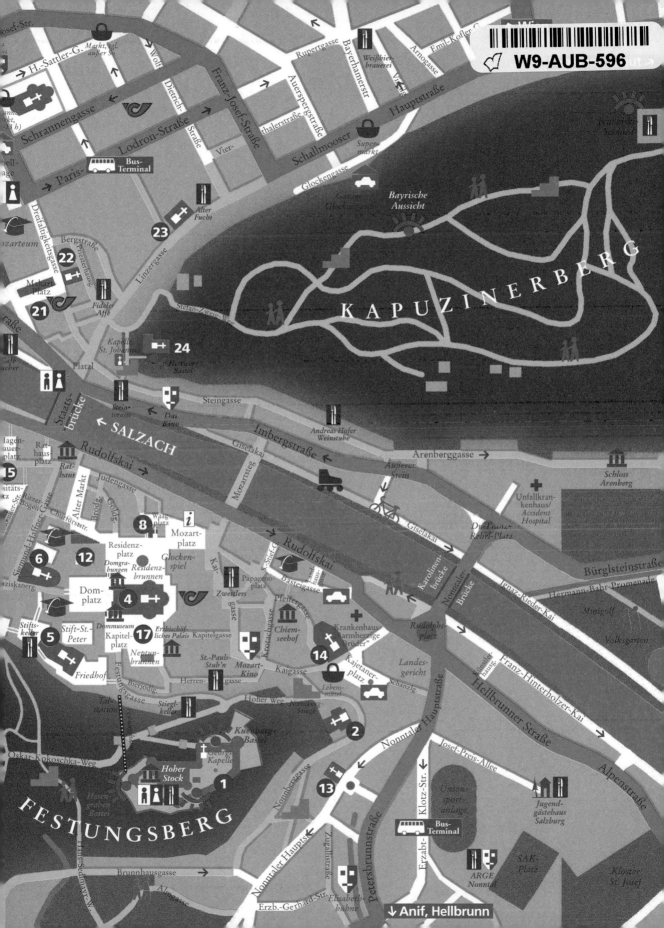

# Salzburg

From the City of Mozart
to the Salzburg Province and
the Salzkammergut Lake District

Book with 112 pages
and more than 400 pictures
Produced by Bernhard Helminger

*Colorama*
*Verlag Salzburg*

# Imprint

**Concept, Text and Layout:**
Bernhard Helminger

ISBN 3-901988-11-4

**Our Homepage:** www.colorama.at; **Tele-
phone:** (0662) 840899–0; **Fax:** DW 44;

**Photos:** Oskar Anrather, Lothar Beckel,
Luigi Caputo, Marcus Hanke, Bernhard
Helminger, Hansjörg Murenwald, Vladis-
law Roubtsov, Wolfgang Retter, Wolfgang
Weinhäupl.

**Pre-Press:** Gordon Feil, Bernhard Helminger, Christian Schober.

**English Translation:** Bernhard Helminger
**Proof Reading:** Sylvia Herites

**Print:** Colordruck Salzburg GmbH

**Printed in Austria**

Please note that this book is also avail-
able in German, Italian, French, Spanish,
Japanese and Russian!

# Contents

A lot of memorials in Salzburg—like this marble relief on Hohensalzburg Fortress—remind of the Founder of the City, Saint Rupert (picture above).

**Celtic Discovery** (picture above right): Golden Celtic Ship from the 4th century BC—on display in the Celtic Museum in Hallein.

**Roman Discovery** (picture in the middle): This 1.800 year old bronze statue symbolizing a bull was found in 1943 near the State Brigde.

**The oldest documented picture** of the City of Salzburg shows its appearance around the year 1460 (to the right).

# Celts, Romans and a Bishop on the Road: The History of Salzburg

Climate, location and the rich soil of the Salzburg basin were the ideal conditions that lured the first settlers to the area, dating back to the early Stone Age (4000–1900 B.C.). The biggest settlement was situated on the Rainberg, one of Salzburg's city mountains. It is believed that the salt-mining on the Dürrnberg Mountain near Hallein began around 700 B.C. and reached a peak after the Celts arrived in the area 400 years B.C. The "white gold" from the Dürrnberg rewarded the region with great prosperity. In the 4th century B.C., the Celts joined forces with the Kingdom of Noricum.

The Romans occupied Noricum in the year 15 B.C. and founded the city of Juvavum. It was the first Roman settlement north of the Alps, raised to the status of a municipality, and developed into an important center of traffic and administration. This golden age came to an end with the Markomanian Wars (160–180). As a result, the city was gradually taken over by tribes of Germanic Bavarians, and with the decline of the Roman Empire (476), sunk into 200 years of oblivion.

In 696, the Franconian Bishop Rupert settled in Salzburg and established St. Peter's Monastery. A convent on the Nonnberg was founded around 700 and Rupert installed his niece Erentrudis as the first abbess. In 739, St. Boniface reorganized the Bavarian church and established the diocese of Salzburg. St. Virgil, originally from Ireland, arrived in Salzburg in 746 and was appointed bishop in 749. He began with the construction of the first cathedral in 767. At its consecration in 774 on St. Rupert's Day (September 24th), Rupert's relics were transferred to the new basilica. In St. Boniface's biography, Salzburg was officially mentioned for the first time. In 798, Charlemagne raised the status of Salzburg to archbishopric and its first archbishop was Arno (785–821), St. Virgil's successor.

200 years later, the dual authority of bishop and abbot was separated, thereby disuniting St. Peter's Abbey from the archbishopric. Henceforth, the archbishop would be elected from amongst the members of the cathedral chapter. In 996, Emperor Otto III granted Salzburg market, tax and coining rights. During the Investiture Controversy (1066–88), Archbishop Gebhard began the construction of the Hohensalzburg and Hohenwerfen Fortresses.

On his quest to conquer Europe, Emperor Friedrich Barbarossa casted a calculated eye on the small archbishopric. When he met with resistance, he had the town burned down in 1167. A reconstruction of the city took place under the reign of Konrad III von Wittelsbach (1177–1200) who also restored the heavily damaged cathedral rendering it even larger than today's.

Leonhard
1498–1519

Matthäus
1519–1540

Max Gandolf
1668–1687

**The most eminent Archbishops of the New Age:**

**Leonhard von Keutschach** enlarged the Hohensalzburg Fortress almost to its present shape. The only authentic portrait of Leonhard is on a gold coin from 1513.

In 1525, rebelling peasants lay siege to Prince-Archbishop **Matthäus Lang von Wellenburg**—confined to the Hohensalzburg Fortress—for 14 weeks. A Swabian army broke the uprising and therewith averted an early secularisation of Salzburg.

No archbishop shaped today's façade of Salzburg more than **Wolf Dietrich von Raitenau.** He erected Mirabell Palace. He demolished the cathedral and many houses around it to create the spacious squares and his residences. Yet, he didn't always find applause for his moves. His powerful enemies made him spend the last years of his life jailed in the Hohensalzburg Fortress.

**Markus Sittikus** hired Italian architect Santino Solari to plan and erect today's cathedral and Hellbrunn Palace.

Wolf Dietrich
1587–1612

Markus
1612–1619

Leopold
1727–1744

Siegmund
1753–1771

Hieronymus
1772–1803

**Paris Graf Lodron** founded the University and is known as the "Father of the Fatherland", today. The Thirty Years War threatened Salzburg, but through his clever foreign policies and his mighty fortification walls Salzburg remained a haven of peace.

**Max Gandolf von Kuenburg** completed the building process of the Hohensalzburg Fortress. He erected the large bastion to the north.

**Johann Ernst Graf von Thun** invited the architect Johann Bernhard Fischer von Erlach to Salzburg. Under his tutelage, the baroque style developed into the harmonious vision that lends the city its fame. One of the most significant architectural creations is the Collegiate Church.

**Leopold Anton Freiherr von Firmian** erected Leopoldskron Palace. In 1731, he expelled 20.000 Protestants—a sad chapter in the history of Salzburg!

**Siegmund Graf von Schrattenbach** was a sponsor of the young Wolfgang Amadeus Mozart.

His successor, **Hieronymus Graf Colloredo,** dismissed Mozart. He was the last archbishop with worldly power as Salzburg lost its autonomy in 1803.

Paris Lodron
1619–1653

Johann
1687–1709

In 1816, after interludes under Bavarian and French control, Salzburg was finally incorporated into the Austrian Empire.

In 1818, Joseph Mohr und Franz Xaver Gruber wrote the Christmas carol "Silent night, holy night" in Oberndorf near Salzburg. The first Mozart festival was celebrated in 1842 in the context of the inauguration of the Mozart monument.

Emperor Franz Joseph I. opened the railway lines to Vienna and Munich in 1860. The fortification walls dating back to the Thirty Years War were pulled down, the city explored a massive economic boost and tourism began. In 1870, the International Foundation Trust "Mozarteum" was founded und Mozart's Birthplace became a museum.

The railway line that connects Salzburg with the city of Villach, 160 kilometers south, was opened in 1909. In World War One (1914–18), Salzburg troups were engaged in Russia and Italy and suffered massive losses. After the war, the First Republic of Austria was proclaimed. This event was followed by the founding of the Salzburg Festival in 1920.

**Johann Michael Sattler** painted his 26-meter-wide Salzburg panorama in 1825. The art work will be on display in the New Residence Building from summer 2004 (above).

**Music sheet "Silent Night, Holy Night"** written in 1818 (to the right).

**Historic Cathedral Square** (Page 11, below): The first „Jedermann"-performance in 1920; bomb attack in 1944.

**Salzburg in 1553** (page 12): The fortress resembles the today's version whereas the large cathedral burned down in 1598.

## World War Two (1939–45):

Austria was annexed to the German Empire in 1938. The invasion of Poland in 1939 started World War Two. Salzburg was bombed from the air sixteen times in 1944, the dome of the cathedral collapsed on October 16th. Many Salzburg soldiers lost their lives in Russia. In May 1945, Salzburg was turned over to US troops without struggle. The Americans remained here for 10 years. The International Treaty that established the Second Republic of Austria was signed on May 15th, 1955.

## Salzburg after World War Two

In 1960, the Large Festival Hall was opened. Thanks to the maestros Karl Böhm und Herbert von Karajan, the Salzburg Festival became the world's leading festival for classical music and performing arts. Austria joined the European Union in 1995. In November 2000, a cable-railway catastrophy on the Kitzsteinhorn Mountain in the Salzburg Province of Pinzgau took 155 lives. This was the worst state tragedy (in times of peace) next to a landslide in 1669 that killed 220 people.

# Hohensalzburg Fortress: Most Important Landmark of City and Province

During the Investiture Controversy between the Emperor and the Pope, Archbishop Gebhard found himself in danger. A faithful follower of the Pope, he feared revenge from a majority of the overlords of southern Germany, who were on the Emperor's side. Therefore in 1077, he began building three castles in his archbishopric: Hohenwerfen (in the Salzburg district Pongau), Friesach (in Carinthia) and Hohensalzburg.

Hohensalzburg is the largest and best preserved medieval fortress. Over a period of 600 years it was expanded and further developed until attaining its present appearance. The greatest expansion was made under Archbishop Leonhard von Keutschach. He had the main building of the castle, the Hoher Stock, enlarged and he designed and furnished the resplendent state rooms on the third floor. In 1525, his successor Matthäus Lang von Wellenburg (1519–1540) was besieged in his fortress for 14 weeks and later liberated by a Swabian army.

During the Thirty Years War, Archbishop Paris Graf von Lodron (1619–1653) had mighty fortification walls built around Salzburg and included the Hohensalzburg in his defense concept. The huge Hasengraben Bastion on the west side dates back to this period. The danger of a Turkish invasion increased in the 17th century. Therefore, Archbishop Max Gandolph von Kuenburg (1668–1687) had the great bastion on the north side built—the last significant enlargement of the fortress.

**The Hohensalzburg Fortress** as it can be seen from the Capuchin Mountain (above).

Page 15: **The southern façade of the fortress** in the four seasons (pictures in the bar to the left); **Hohensalzburg Fortress** seen from the Gaisberg Mountain (in the mist; above right) and from Maria Plain Pilgrimage Church (below right).

**In this wooden box on top of the castlewall,** the "Salzburg Bull"—an organ built around 1500—is set up (above).

**The Funicular** was opened in 1892 (above right). In the early 1960's, an electrical system was installed (in the middle to the right). Further changes were made in 1990 (below right).

Inside and outside **St. George's Chapel** (pictures above left and in the middle).

No archbishop had more elements of today's fortress erected than **Leonhard von Keutschach.** To call attention on himself, he commissioned a marble relief portrait on the side wall of St. George's Chapel (above right).

**The Courtyard** (large picture in the middle).

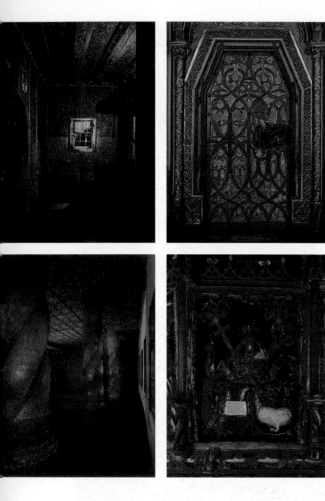

**The State Apartments:**

**The Golden Chamber** (right) with its ceramic-tiled heating stove dating from 1501.

**More Art Treasures** (pictures above, clockwise): Door to the Golden Chamber; focusing the ceramic-tiled stove: The coat of arms of Leonhard von Keutschach; four columns in the Golden Hall, made of "Adnet" marble; library.

The **"Salzburg Bull"** (above) is considered to be the oldest working gothic organ in the world.

**Tapestry** depicting the coat of arms of Archbishop Wolf Dietrich von Raitenau (in the middle, left).

**The Private Chapel of Leonhard von Keutschach** (in the middle, right) with richly ornamented star vault.

**The Gold Coins** were minted between 1350 and 1400 and later hidden on the fortress grounds— maybe because of riots. Found in 1998 by accident.

**The Fortress Museum:**

**Romanesque Arcade Window** (above), richly ornamented with paintings from the 12<sup>th</sup> century; collection of historic weapons and furniture (pictures to the left).

# „Spiritual" Cathedral and "Secular" Residence: The Buildings of the Principality

The first Cathedral at this location was constructed by the Irish bishop St. Virgil (746–784). Excavations show that this church with three naves was 66 meters long and 33 meters wide.

Under the auspices of Archbishop Cardinal Konrad III von Wittelsbach (1177–1183) a remarkable transformation followed. The Cathedral emerged as a structure with five naves and a length of 112 meters. The dimensions of the present-day house of God were thereby markedly surpassed. The eighth catastrophic fire in the history of the Cathedral on December 11th, 1598, irrevocably sealed its fate. Archbishop Wolf Dietrich von Raitenau could only have the ruins pulled down.

His successor Archbishop Markus Sittikus ordered his court architect, the northern Italian Santino Solari, to design the new Cathedral with the same measurements we find today (length: 99 meters, hight: 68 meters, nave width: 45 meters). The late Renaissance building with baroque character was started in 1614 and, after only fourteen years of construction, was completed and consecrated by Archbishop Paris Lodron. The towers were given their present shape during the reign of his successor, Archbishop Guidobald Thun. On October 16th, 1944, the church was struck by a bomb dropped by the US Air Force. The dome collapsed and the interior was badly damaged.

**The Statues at the cathedral façade** (top, left) made of marble from the Untersberg Mountain: Top tier: Jesus (see picture top, right); beneath: Moses and Elijah; on the balcony of the first floor: The four evangelists; ground floor: The saints Rupert, Peter, Paul and Virgil.

**The Bronze Doors at the entrance** (bottom, right) were made in 1957 and 1958. They symbolize (left to right) Faith (Toni Schneider-Manzell), Charity (Giacomo Manzù), and Hope (Ewald Mataré).

**The High Altar** (top) is a joint venture of those two artists who were engaged the most with the construction of the Cathedral: The architect Santino Solari provided the baroque design, Donato Mascagni created the high altar painting "Resurrection of Christ".

**The Cupola** (bottom, right): Donato Mascagni and his student Ignazio Solari painted most of the frescos. An artist group led by Giuseppe Bassarino executed the stucco work.

**The Cathedral is equipped with five organs** (above). In the 1980's, new mechanics were inserted in the baroque body of the main organ (picture in the middle, right).

**The Baptismal Font** (in the middle) is one of the Cathedral's greatest historical art treasures. It was cast in 1321 by Meister Heinrich. The copper lions of the socles date back to the 12th century.

**The Ceiling Paintings of the "Beautiful Gallery"** (top, right) were produced by Johann Michael Rottmayr (1654–1730). **More Resplendent Halls:** Conference Room (top, left), Audience Room (in the middle, right).

**The Old Residence Building** (in the middle, left) takes the western edge of Residence Square.

**The Residence Gallery** dedicates itself to European Graphic Art of the 16th to 19th century (picture to the right: Peter Paul Rubens, 1577–1640, "Girl with satyr and fruit basket").

**The Residence Fountain** was erected between 1658 and 1661 and is the largest baroque fountain outside Italy (top, left).

**The New Residence Building** with the "Glockenspiel" (carillon, top picture) is situated opposite the Old Residence Building. The 35 bells, cast by Melchior de Haze (1688/89) in Antwerp, were originally meant for a bell tower in Breda, unfortunately destroyed by fire. Archbishop Johann Ernst Thun bought the bells in 1694 and his watchmaker, Jeremias Sauter, built the tricky mechanism (to the left).

# „Ora et labora"
# The Benedictines: Founders of Today's Salzburg

It's a ten-minute-walk from St. Peter's Abbey to the nunnery on Nonnberg Mountain, but when the history of Salzburg is the subject, these two places belong together.

The occupation by the Romans and ensuing desertion left the city depopulated and in ruins. It began to flourish with the founding of St. Peter's by St. Rupert in 696, eventually achieving its present splendor and rank. Today, St. Peter's is the oldest surviving Benedictine cloister north of the Alps. The monastery church was built as a romanesque basilica between 1130 and 1143 and redecorated in late baroque style in the 18th century. Paintings on a column in the main nave date back to the first building period of the church. They emphasize that St. Peter's is the only romanesque church of Salzburg.

The nunnery on top of the Nonnberg Mountain was founded by St. Rupert in 714. He installed his niece Erentrudis as the first abbess. The red onion steeple of the abbey church can be seen from many places in and around the city.

**The picturesque St. Peter's Cemetery** has kept its present appearance since 1627 and is the city's most atmospheric spot. Innumerable personalities, important with regard to Salzburg history, are buried here. The walk through the catacombs leads to the St. Gertraud's and the St. Maximus' Chapels (above). It is still a subject to science, but perhaps even the Romans used these caves and the place itself for funerals.

**Examples of medieval forgery art work** can be found in St. Peter's (above right) as well as Nonnberg Abbey (in the middle, right).

**The interior of St. Peter´s and Nonnberg Abbey Churches:** Whereas the monks of St. Peter's lent their house of God a late baroque design in 1754 (above, left), the sisters of Nonnberg conserved the original gothic decoration (picture to the right).

Picture page 36: Nonnberg Abbey Church—christianed in 1475—with its prominent red onion steeple.

# "Rome of the North" – the Churches of Salzburg

Two dozen churches are situated in the area of the Old Town of Salzburg. That's why the city snatched the honorable surname "Rome of the North". "The City of Baroque" is another term associated with Salzburg as many of the sacral buildings were either erected in the Baroque period or—like some older churches such as St. Peter's—remodeled following the ideas of that conceptualism.

A baroque masterpiece and one of the most beautiful baroque buildings in central Europe is the Collegiate or University Church built by the Viennese architect Johann Bernhard Fischer von Erlach. The same architect created Holy Trinity and St. Marc's Churches.

Another master architect was Giovanni Gaspare Zuccalli who made a mark on Salzburg with St. Cajetan's and St. Erhard's Churches. The latter can be found in the suburb of Nonntal. Churches that were redesigned in baroque style include St. Michael's on Residenzplatz Square, St. Augustine's Church in the suburb of Mülln and St. Sebastian's Church in Linzergasse Lane.

Imposing gothic structures are: The steeple of Franciscan Church, the church of the Nonnberg nunnery, St. George's Church in the Hohensalzburg Fortress and St. Blaise's Church which can be found at the end of Getreidegasse lane.

**Collegiate Church** (pictures this page): The golden age of the Baroque style in Salzburg occurred under the rule of Archbishop Johann Ernst Graf Thun (1687–1709). He had this basilica built for the University by the architect Fisher von Erlach between 1696 and 1707. It is often referred to as the University Church by many of the city's residents.

**The Franciscan Church** (above, left) is one of the oldest buildings in the festival city. It is assumed that a baptismal chapel or synodical church stood here already in the early 8th century, even before St. Virgil's cathedral. What is certain is this: The late Romanesque nave dates back to the 12th century and the Choir to the first half of the 15th (above, right). The steeple, originally Gothic, later built in Baroque style was redone in Neo-gothic style in 1866/67 (above). The statue of Madonna on the high altar was created by Michael Pacher (1495/98, picture above, in the middle).

This tricky perspective makes **St. Michael's Church** seem bigger than the cathedral (above, left). In reality though, this little church is always a bit underexposed due to the high number of large spirtual buildings in Salzburg. However, it's by no means insignificant: Its genesis goes back to the 8th century which makes it the oldest parish church in the city. It was confered into today's appearance in 1776 (picture above, right: steeple of St. Michael's).

**St. John on Imberg Mountain** (Bild rechts): A stairway beginning in Steingasse Street—just a stone's throw from Staatsbrücke Bridge—leads to another little church. As well as St. Michael's, St. John's is also of Romanesque origin and was mentioned for the first time in 1319.

**St. Marc's Church** (above, left) and **Holy Trinity Church** (above, in the middle)—with its large fresco on the dome (in the middle, left)— were both erected by Johann Bernhard Fischer von Erlach.

In 1350, **St. Blaise's Church** (above, right) was built for the next door hospital that operated between 1327 and 1898. The arcaded courtyard of this former hospital (large picture) is the one of few traces the Renaissance—the architectural style dominant in the late 16th century —left in Salzburg. Another baroque church, **Augustinian Church,** is situated in the quarter Mülln (to the left).

In the "Rome of the North" it doesn't surprise us that the quarters Kaiviertel and Nonntal (below, left with red steeple of Nonnberg Abbey) have churches as landmarks. Both are baroque masterpieces by the Swiss architect Caspar Zuccalli and built between 1685 and 1700: **St. Cajetan's Church** (above, left) and **St. Erhard's Church** (above, right).

A hidden treasure of baroque style is the altar painting by Paul Troger (picture below, right) in St. Cajetan's Church.

**Abbey Church of the Capuchin Monastery:** Over the roofs of the burgher houses on the right Salzach river bank—half way up the Capuchin Mountain (above, left)—Archbishop Wolf Dietrich built a monastery for the Capuchins in 1602 (above, right). The path that passed the cloister starts at Linzergasse Street and leads up to the top of the highest city mountain (picture to the left).

**St. Sebastian's Cemetery**—founded in 1499—
was in Wolf Dietrich's time the main cemetery of the city. The ground plan resembles
an Italian style "campo santo". Rising in the
middle of the cemetery is the mosaic-deco-
rated St. Gabriel's Chapel, Wolf Dietrich's
mausoleum which he had built during his
lifetime (picture in the middle, left).

# Salzburg "on foot": The Streets and Squares of the Old Town

Salzburg owes the spacious squares around the cathedral—Residence-, Cathedral- and Kapitel ("Chapter"-) Square—to archbishop Wolf Dietrich. Between 1588 and 1604, he had dozens of burgher houses demolished and moved the cathedral cemetery to the other side of the river to Linzergasse Lane (St. Sebastian's cemetery). His master builder Vincenzo Scamozzi—at that time a world star of architecture who also left his mark on Piazza di S. Marco in Venice—believed in the idea that a "perfect city" should have five large town squares. Following this claim, the small German city of Salzburg changed into an Italian style principality.

Adding Mozart and University Squares, the "Alter Markt" Square as well as the square in front of the Festival Complex, today's Salzburg consists of no less than seven squares which lend the city a unique atmosphere.

A stroll through the narrow lanes of the Old Town makes you feel taken back to the Middle Ages. Especially those between Residence Square and the Salzach River have kept their character. The smallest of all—Döllerergässchen—runs behind the former house of justice (Waagplatz Square No. 1). The first bread market was in Brodgasse and in Judengasse ("Lane of the jews"), a synagog was situated.

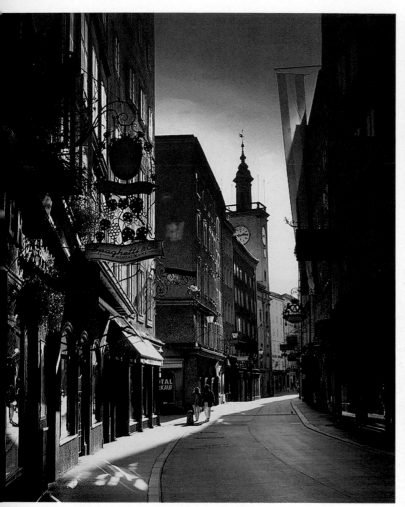

**"Getreidegasse",** the commercial center of the city, has changed a lot in the last decade. Shopping centers on the outskirts are giving this historical thoroughfare tough competition. The shop and business signs of partly gilded wrought iron originated during the Middle Ages, a time of illiteracy. The inner courtyards of some of the houses are well worth seeing. Something fun and distinctive to Salzburg are the passageways (like the "Jewelry passage") connecting Getreidegasse with its parallel line of streets.

**"Linzergasse"** (above, left) leads from the Staatsbrücke Bridge eastwards. It was once the main passage way towards Vienna and Linz.

You can reach **"Goldgasse"** (below, left) across Residenzplatz Square. This narrow street owes its name to a number of gold smiths who lived and worked here centuries ago.

**"Herrengasse"** (Gentlemen's street, above, right) is named after (male) executives who were in the archbishop's service and inhabited house No. 8.

**"Steingasse"** (stone street) runs parallel to the Salzach River. Before the broad road on the river bank was built a century ago, this narrow street was the only passage between river and Capuchin Mountain.

The **"Alter Markt"** (old market square, above, left): In the middle ages, the main market was situated here. In 1857, it moved to **University Square** (above, right) only a stone's throw away, where it can still be found today.

**Looking down from the Fortress** (in the middle, right): To the south of the Cathedral, the space today occupied by Chapter Square, a cloister was once situated. **The Neptune Fountain** on the same square (to the left) was created by Anton Pfaffinger in 1732.

**Mozart Monument on Mozart Square** (above): The author Julius Schilling—a newcomer to Salzburg—gave the inspiration for a Mozart Monument in 1835. It was inaugurated seven years later, in September 1842.

**"Pferdeschwemme"** (horse pond, picture to the right) on Herbert von Karajan Square was built in 1695 by Fischer von Erlach and served as the watering-place for the archbishop's riding stables. The statue of the "horse tamer" was created by the sculptor Michael Bernhard Mandl.

# Mirabell: Archbishop Wolf Dietrich and a Palace dedicated to his Courtesan

The palace of Mirabell—originally called "Altenau"— was built in 1606 on the behalf of Prince-Archbishop Wolf Dietrich for his beloved Salome Alt and their children. Wolf Dietrich's successor renamed the Palace "Mirabell" (beautiful sight). It was reconstructed under Lukas von Hildebrandt from 1721 to 1727, but much of it burned down in the year 1818.

When it was constructed anew the tower (see engraving on page 56) had to be demolished and the façade was simplified following the ideas of the classicism. In 1866, the property was communized and today accomodates the seat of the city administration.

The gardens were designed in their present state by Fischer von Erlach. Last constructional changes were executed in 1730, that's why Mirabell today stands for a perfect and pure example of a baroque park. More art work of this style can be seen in the Baroque Museum next to the conservatory. It was opened in 1973 and is certainly worth a side-glance!

**This Breathtaking View** of the Mirabell Gardens and the Old Town can be enjoyed from the mayor's office (picture to the right).

**The Fountain in the Center of the Park** is surrounded by four large marble statue groupings. In conjunction with mythological figures, they symbolize the four elements. The statue "Hercules struggles with Anteus" symbolizes the air (picture above). Ottavio Mosto created the sculptures in 1690.

**The Façade of Mirabell Palace** was once far more pumpous (picture above: Engraving by F. A. Danreiter, 1727, courtesy of Salzburg Baroque Museum).

A fire in 1818 led to the simple appearance of today (picture to the right).

**Gilded Stucco Work and Splendid Marble**
made the Marmorsaal (marble hall) one of
the most beautiful wedding halls in the world
(picture above).

This part of Mirabell Palace—with the
**Angels' staircase** by Raphael Donner (picture
to the left)—survived the fire of 1818 and
gives us an idea how splendid the palace
must have been.

# Mozart in Salzburg: The City and its Greatest Son

The most frequently visited place In the city is the modest house in Getreidegasse in which Wolfgang Amadeus Mozart was born. His father Leopold (1719–1787)—vice-director of music in the services of the archbishop—lived with his wife Anna Maria Walburga on the fourth (respectively: third) floor. Seven children were born in this house, but only two survived babyhood: Maria Anna Walburga (Nannerl), born in 1751, and Wolfgang Amadeus, born on 27th of January 1756. He lived here until the age of seventeen, except of course, when he was on a tour.

This birthplace is like a pilgrim's shrine to lovers of Mozart—in high season up to 5000 people visit the museum every day. The highlight is the Mozarts' apartment on the fourth (respectively: third) floor where the Mozarts' kitchen, original instruments, letters and family portraits are exhibited.

A walk taken in Mozart's footsteps should lead to Mozarts' Residence on the right bank of the river, where Wolfgang Amadeus—when in Salzburg—resided between 1773 and 1780.

**The Mozart Family:** Father Leopold (1719–1787); mother Anna Maria (1720–1778); sister Nannerl (top pictures from left to right); family portrait from 1782 (in the middle, left; a portait of the mother who had died four years earlier can be seen in the frame behind the piano); Wolfgang Amadeus (in the middle, right; most authentic of all Mozart portraits, painted 1789); his wife Constanze (to the right).

**Mozart's Birthplace** (above): In 1880, the International Foundation Trust "Mozarteum" converted the Mozart apartment into a museum and managed to buy the house in 1917.

During Mozart's lifetime, a fish market was held on the square in front of the Mozart house. The fountain was removed in 1873 (picture to the left).

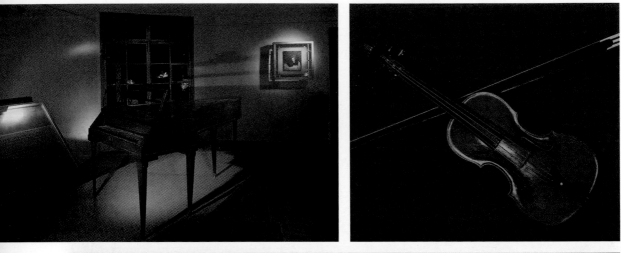

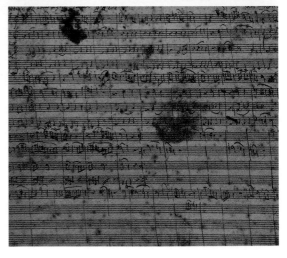

**The Four-Room Apartment** is the highlight of the Mozart Museum: Kitchen, closet, living room, bedroom and office. Here, portraits, instruments, music sheets and personal belongings of the family are on display.

Top pictures: His pianoforte from the Viennese Walter Company, his childhood violin. In the middle: Living room with family portraits. To the right: Autograph "Adagio for Englishhorn".

Between 1773 and 1780, Wolfgang Amadeus stayed in the **Family Residence on Makartplatz Square** when in Salzburg (above). His father lived in the flat until his death in 1787. From 1994 until 1996 the house, having been damaged in WW II and then cleared away, was finally reconstructed in its original state (bottom, right). Of all the historical rooms, it was only possible to restore the Dancing-Master's Hall, Mozart's concert hall (bottom picture to the left).

# Festival Time: Five Weeks in a Permanent State of Excitement

The Salzburg Festival had its beginnings in the Mozart festivals of the 19th century. In 1842, on the occasion of the unveiling of the Mozart memorial, a music festival was given, and then repeated at irregular intervals. The Viennese theatrical expert, Max Reinhardt, established the Salzburg Festival Community in 1917 to which Richard Strauss, Franz Schalk and Hugo von Hofmannsthal also belonged. Eventually in 1920 the big day came and for the Salzburg Festival it was fortunately: "Curtain Call!"

In 1920—the year the Festival was founded —it was the earnest intention of planners to build the Festival Hall in Hellbrunn. At that time, however, like nowadays, grand ideas fizzle out for lack of money and the Festival was moved "temporarily" into the archbishops' former riding stables. As you know, the move became a permanent arrangement: The front of Max Reinhardt Square by the Mönchsberg cliffs and the entire Hofstallgasse were taken over by all three Festival theaters.

**"Hofstallgasse"** (top, left) is occupied by the sublime festival audience from mid July to the end of August. Hundreds of sneakers try to catch a glimpse of a VIP like Prince Charles (with Camilla) who was a guest in 2003.

**This Portal**—created by famous architect Fischer von Erlach—separates the ticketholders from the less fortunate ones (picture in the middle, left).

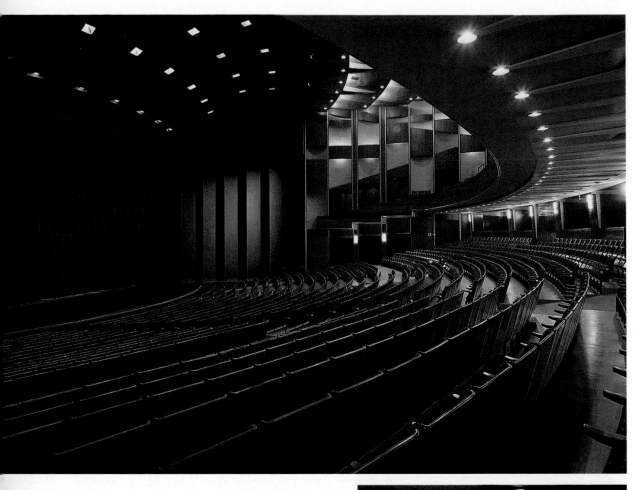

**The Large Festivall Hall** (above) was opened in 1960. 50.000 cubic meters of rock were blasted out of the Mönchsberg Mountain in order to make room for a 100 meter wide, 60 meter high, 65 meter deep playhall. The auditorium holds 2.400 persons. In the year of the opening, the technical furnishings were regarded with great respect and set an example for modern stage building, serving as a model for the Opera Hall in Sydney (picture to the right: "Don Giovanni" production of 1987).

**"Jedermann"**—a play written by Hugo von Hofmanns-thal—was performed for the first time on Cathedral Square in 1920. Peter Simonischek (in the title role, right) and Veronica Ferres (as his courtesan, left) star in the current production that was introduced in 2002 (top, right).

**The Rock Riding School** (pictures to the left) has existed since the 17th century when the conglomerate rock was cut out as building material for the cathedral. The 96 arcades were created during the reign of Archibishop Johann Ernst Thun in 1693.

# Arctic Coldness, Tropical Heat: The Salzburg Climate has everything to offer!

The weather is the locals' most favorite subject of conversation and the subalpine climate gives them a lot to talk about!

The northern alpine upland is a region where the seasons vary in a striking way. Locals have to adjust to the fact that the way of life in summer is totally different to that in the cold season. In winter, the arctic coldness makes temperatures drop as low as minus 20° C (minus 4° F). If the weather changes and a lively breeze from the south is determining, even in winter, up to plus 15° C (59° F) are possible.

In the same way, the weather in summer is sometimes unpredictable as well. The record breaking summer of 2003 passed the 30 degree level (86° Fahrenheit) on 29 days! Unbelieveable! One year earlier, however, in the midsummer month of August the richest rainfalls of all times occured.

The following photo portrait illustrates that the most beautiful seasons are spring and fall. A weather phenomenon Salzburg is famous for can be observed in all seasons: A very light rain called "Schnürlregen" (string rain).

**Spring:** Blooming magnolias in front of Holy Trinity Church (above, left); St. Peter's Cemetery (above, right); the Krauthügel Hill on the rear side of the Hohensalzburg Fortress (below, left); "Palmbuschen" (Palm Sunday Bunches), an old Christian practice on the last sunday before easter (below, right); Spring all around Nonnberg Abbey, whereas on Untersberg Mountain it is still winter (large picture page 73).

**Summer:** The "Fackeltanz" (torch-dance) on Residence Square traditionally amplifies the opening cere-mony of the Salzburg Festival (above, left); at night in front of the Café Tomaselli (above, right); "sweating" horse of the Residenzbrunnen Fountain (below, left); well-dressed Festival guests in Getreidegasse Lane (below, right); the famous terrace café on top of Hotel Stein near Staatsbrücke Bridge (page 75).

**Fall:** Walking around in Mirabell Gardens (above, left); church towers in the autumn mist (above, right); parkgrounds at Hellbrunn Palace, all winter preparations already done (below left); fall atmosphere at the Salzach River (below, right); looking down from the Humboldt Terrace towards the Old Town of Salzburg (large picture page 77).

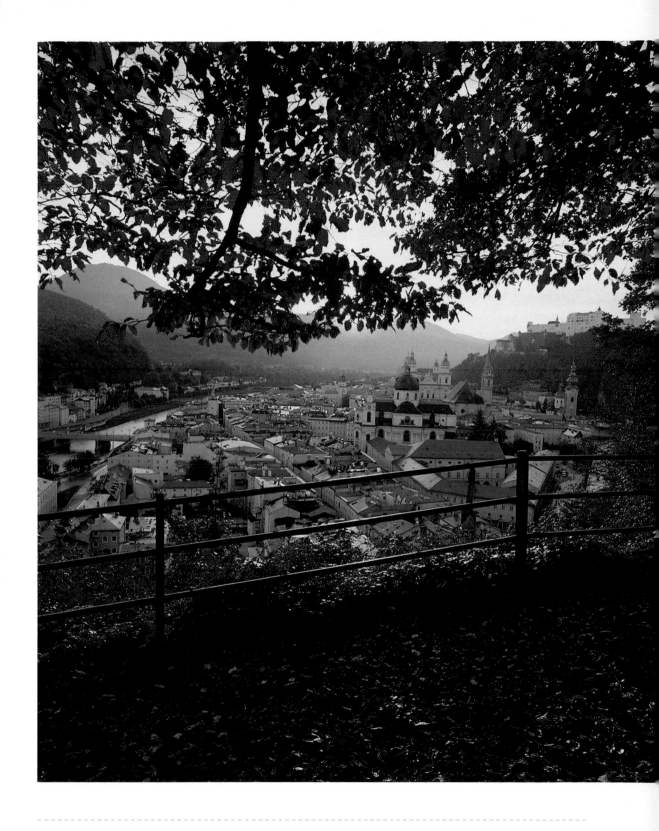

**Winter:** Hotel Mönchstein, a fairy tale castle on the Mönchsberg Mountain above the Mülln Quarter (top, left); winter morning over the City of Mozart (top, right); Salzburg Christmas Market (below, left); looking down from Capuchin Mountain towards Hohensalzburg Fortress (below, right); a perfect winter day: To see snow on the steep roof of Franciscan Church is a rare sight (large picture page 79).

# The Beautiful City without its Picturesque Surroundings? Inconceivable!

Wealthy archbishops and important artists left Salzburg with a unique worldwide cultural heritage. The question is why did St. Rupert chose Salzburg as his bishopric? Why did famous architects prefer to work here? And, why did Max Reinhardt decide to fulfill his dreams of the Festival here, along the Salzach River? The answer lies, without doubt, in the breathtaking beauty of the surrounding areas which leaves no guest untouched.

The palaces built by the prince-archbishops such as Leopoldskron, Klessheim or Hellbrunn are highlights of the vicinities. But there is more: The lake district to the North, the alpine upland to the South, the Berchtesgaden county with Lake Königssee to the West and the Salzkammergut Lake District to the East, no matter where you cross the border of the Salzburg basin, you will find a landscape that makes the City of Mozart a charming composition of art, culture and nature.

**Leopoldskron Palace** was constructed by Archbishop Leopold Anton Firmian (1724–1744) for his relatives. It remained, until 1837, in his family's possession until it changed owners several times. Even the founder of the Salzburg Festival, Max Reinhardt, owned the palace before it was bought by an American Institute in 1958. The rococo building lies south of Hohensalzburg fortress, only a few minutes on foot from the inner city. Its romantic location on a large pond is still used by international filmmakers (e. g. "The Sound of Music").

**Klessheim Palace** (above) is a good example of high-baroque architecture. The architectural dreams of Archbishop Thun were realized in this structure which was built from 1700 to 1709 by the star architect of that time, Johann Bernhard Fischer von Erlach.

**Anif Castle** (to the left), a charming romantic castle, surrounded by a moat, was constructed from 1838 to 1814 on the site of an older building. Now, privately owned, the entire area is closed off; it's possible, however, to catch a glance of this lovely sight over the castle wall.

**Renaissance Hellbrunn Palace** was erected under the rule of Archbishop Markus Sittikus from 1613 to 1619 (above: main façade with castle courtyard; beneath: rear side with star pond). Donato Mascagni's wall paintings in the Grand Hall are an art-historic treasure (to the right). Highlight of every visit are the Trick Water Fountains where wet surprises are on the agenda (pictures page 85).

**Maria Plain:** Due to the unique location on Plainberg Mountain, the baroque church can be seen from almost anywhere in the city. The view from Maria Plain of the Salzburg basin is breathtaking. G. A. Dario built the church from 1671 to 1674. A dignified place to keep a painting of Maria was created. The wonderworking image of Maria with her child, encircled in a silver halo, can be admired at the high altar. It is said that the picture survived a great fire in 1633. Stations of the cross are found below the church.

**Hallein** (above) with its 15.000 inhabitants is the second largest city in Salzburg Province. Finds from the celtic settlement on the Dürrnberg Mountain near Hallein can be seen in the Celtic Museum. Another highlight is the guided tour through the former salt mines. The grave of Franz Xaver Gruber, the composer of "Silent Night, Holy Night", can be found on the cemetery (above, right). Another dedication to this christmas carol is **a Chapel in the Town of Oberndorf** (bottom). Here, the song was composed in 1818.

**Trumer Seenland Lake District:** A lovely country-side lies northwest of the city of Salzburg where a number of lakes are situated among lush and verdant hills and meadows that produce perfect conditions for agriculture. **The Village of Mattsee** (to the right) is located on the lake of the same name and offers its guest a museum where Bavarian culture can be seen (above, left). The town of Seekirchen is situated on **Lake Wallersee** (in the middle, left).

# The Austrian Emperor Franz Joseph I and the Salzkammergut Lake District

Crystal-clear mountain lakes, jagged rocks, green hills, romantic villages—these are the elements that contribute to the allure of the Salzkammergut. Between 1850 and 1914 the region attracted a celebrity guest: Emperor Franz Joseph I spent his summers here, met his wife Elisabeth and signed the Declaration of War against Serbia in 1914 which marked the beginning of World War One.

Geographically, the Salzkammergut is a difficult term to categorize. The name means literally "salt chamber estates" and referred originally to a former salt-mining territory around the villages of Hallstatt, Ebensee and Gmunden that was owned by the royal Habsburg family. The "white gold" was an important source of revenue for the imperial chamber in Vienna.

Today, it's tourism that keeps the brand "Salzkammergut" alive. The area around Lake Fuschlsee and Lake Wolfgangsee had no connection with the Habsburgs' salt mines and didn't even belong to the Empire until 1816. Today, however, these parts definitely belong to it as well as Hallstatt, the town that defines a prehistoric era (Hallstatt-Era, 800 to 400 B.C.) and the cities of Bad Ischl and Gmunden which all lie in the Province of Upper Austria. The beautiful landscape around Bad Aussee belongs to the Province of Styria.

**Fuschl** (above) is the western gate of the Salzkammergut. The posh village on the lake of the same name was first mentioned in 790, but stayed a sleepy hamlet for centuries. The castle of Fuschl, once a hunting lodge belonging to the archbishops, is now a luxury hotel (picture to the right).

Only a ruin is left of **Wartenfels Castle** that was built in the 13<sup>th</sup> century. It is a 30-minute-walk from Fuschl. The sad condition of the historical landmark, however, doesn't harm the breathtaking view from it (picture page 90).

**St. Gilgen on Lake Wolfgangsee** (above, right) is the birthtown of Mozart's mother. That is why the main square is named after Salzburg's greatest son (above, left) although he has never seen the town. The Zwölferhorn Mountain with its altitude of 1.522 meters is accessible from St. Gilgen thanks to a cable-car.

**Hüttenstein Castle**—within walking distance from St. Gilgen—is located on the banks of Lake Krotensee (in the middle, left).

From the Lake Wolfgangsee village of **Strobl,** a lovely hike leads up to the **Laimeralm Alp** (to the left).

**The Village of St. Wolfgang** (above) owes its fame not only to the fantastic location on the lake, but also to a restaurant on the lake's promenade (above, right) which was also the inspiration for the operetta "The White Horse Inn". A treasure of art history in St. Wolfgang is the Gothic winged altar by Michael Pacher (third picture from top). This wonderful work of wood carving, dating from 1481, can be seen in the parish church. The 130 year-old paddle steamer "Kaiser Franz-Joseph I" (to the right)—in service since 1873—offers the most romantic way to get to St. Wolfgang.

Since 1893, **the Schafberg-Cog-Railway** has taken guests up the 1.782 meter high **Schafberg Mountain.** The steam engines, dating back to the emperor's time, need 50 minutes for the seven kilometer stretch. The Schafberg with its clearly defined peak offers a magnificent view of numerous lakes of the Salzkammergut. On a clear day, the imperial city of Bad Ischl can be seen as well.

**The Town of Mondsee** is dominated architecturally by the mighty Parish Church of St. Michael's (above). The dimensions of this cathedral bear witness to the power of the cloister established in 748 by the Bavarian duke Odilo II and closed down in 1792. The high alter is by Hans Waldburger (1626).

Because of the terrace cafés and cultural events, **the Town Square of Mondsee** (page 97, pictures in the middle) becomes a lively place in summer.
From Lake Mondsee, it's a short distance to the largest of the Salzkammergut lakes, **Lake Attersee** (page 97, bottom left).

**Bad Ischl** owes its present-day reputation as an imperial city and the "heart" of the Salzkammergut to the visits of Emperor Franz Joseph I. (1830–1916) and high-ranking members of the Habsburg dynasty. Dignified guests of the state, like King Wilhelm I. of Prussia (1865), were received at the "Kaiservilla", the Habsburgs' Biedermeier country house (large picture in the middle). The news that Franz Joseph engaged himself in 1853 to Elisabeth (Sissi) can be read in the city chronicles as well.

Additional pictures: Health resort of Bad Ischl (above, left); view into the towncenter (above, right); villa of **Franz Lehár** (1870–1948, to the right), composer of many popular operettas.

Between the shores of the dark Lake Hallstättersee (with boat excursions) and the steep mountainside, lies the charming **Village of Hallstatt** (above). The parish church, Maria Himmelfahrt, dating from 1505, was literally chiseled out of the mountain and has a spendid late gothic winged altar. The Hallstatt people living space is so restricted that the graves have to be cleared after ten years. The skeletons of the dead are kept in the Charnel House.

Rich Celtic findings—dating back to the early Iron Age—can be seen in the Celtic Museum. Even then, salt provided the region with great wealth.

**The City of Gmunden** (picture to the bottom left on page 100 with the Grünberg Mountain cable-car) occupies a splendid piece of land on the banks of Lake Traunsee. The town hall from the 16th century is equipped with a carillon. The bells are made of ceramics (bottom right on page 100). Thanks to a German television series, the lakeside castle became a prime time tourist attraction (large picture on page 100). On board the **Gisela**—a paddle steamer built in 1871 (above, in the middle)—**the Village of Traunkirchen** (above, right: Johannesbergkapelle Chapel) or **the Town of Ebensee** (above, left) can be reached. Another cable-car leads from Ebensee up the Feuerkogel Mountain which offers a great view of the area and the highest peak of this region, the Traunstein Mountain (1.691 meters, large picture).

**Our journey through the Salzkammergut Lake District** began in the nord-west, on Lake Fuschlsee, and ends in the Ausseer Land, the south-eastern part of this region. The work of our photographer Wolfgang Weinhäupl tells everything of the beauty of this countryside. That's why we keep this legend short: **On Lake Grundlsee** (large panorama); **Town of Bad Aussee** (to the right); **Loser Mountain** (page 103, bottom, left); the **Village of Altaussee** on the lake of the same name (page 103, bottom, right).

# Pongau, Pinzgau, Lungau: The Districts of Salzburg "in the Mountain Area"

It's time for a geography lesson: The Province of Salzburg consists of the City of Salzburg plus five districts. Two of those, the Flachgau District and the Tennengau District, lie in the alpine upland around the Salzburg basin. That's why this region is called "Aussergebirg", which means something like "outside the mountain area". "Innergebirg", "in the mountain area", there are the districts Pongau, Pinzgau and Lungau.

In the Middle Ages, Pongau District was an important center for the gold and copper mining industry. Today, the mother lode is tourism. Spotless farming villages like Wagrain, Filzmoos, Kleinarl or Großarl have bloomed into meccas of winter sports. The historical epicenter of Pongau tourism are the hot springs in the Gastein Valley. The towns of Badgastein and Bad Hofgastein are first class health resorts and offer boundless possibilities for destraction to their guests.

Pinzgau District is home of the Hohe Tauern National Park with the highest peaks of the province. Two regions ought to be pointed out: The "Oberpinzgau" covers the Salzach River Valley between the village of Krimml and the picturesque district capital of Zell am See. A paradise for every hiker is the Rauris Valley.

For the smallest district, the Lungau, think "back to basic". The tourism industry is less developed and the relaxed, pristine atmosphere will delight those seeking the calm.

**Our stroll through the mountainous regions** of Salzburg starts in the south-west. This region is situated at the widest distance from the City of Mozart. The **Pinzgau Railway** (in the middle, right) is a romantic alternative to the cartrip if you'd like to reach the **Village of Krimml** (above, right). Here, the highest **waterfalls** of the alps can be seen (above, left). In three levels, the water dashes down 380 meters which makes a 22nd place in the listing of the world's highest. Above the falls, the **Krimmler Achental Valley** is another impressive sight (bottom picture to the right).

The high number of castles in the **Lungau** illustrate how hard-fought this important European passage from the north to the south once was (page 104: **Moosham Castle).**

A rich flora and fauna awaits every visitor to the province of Salzburg. With a little luck one can see **Edelweiss** (top picture to the right), **Ibex** (beneath), **marmot** (top picture to the left) or a **White Head Vulture** (beneath). A more omnipresent sight, however, are **cows,** but only in fall, when they are taken off the alps and back to the farm, they are decorated as beautifully as in our picture to the bottom left.

**The Großglockner Mountain** is the highest peak of Austria. Picture to the right, in the foreground: **Dreiherrnspitze** (3.499 m); left: **Großvenediger** (3.674 m); in the back: **Großglockner** (3.798 m).

The **Großglockner Hochalpenstraße Alpine Road** was built in 1936 and climbs to an altitude of 2.505 meters (above, left). Another masterpiece of engineering are the two **dam walls in the Kaprun Valley.** Erected 1947 to 1955, they hold up to 165 million cubic meters of water (in the middle, left).

**In Pongau: Hohenwerfen Castle** (above); **Mühl-bach,** one of those villages where tourism and the ski industry paved the way to prosperity (in the middle, left); dip into the **Gastein Valley** (in the middle, right); in the **"Malerwinkel" Valley,** close to the village of Badgastein with its thermal springs, famous climber Luis Trenker erected a crucifix (picture on page 111).